LIVING IN COLOR

Achieve Your Best Life by Breaking the Rules

Living In Color

Achieve Your Best Life by Breaking the Rules

Dom Mitchell

DEDICATION

In Loving Memory of Sherry Soth

You affected many in your time on earth with your presence and actions. Never without a smile and always lighting up the room with your energy. You inspired many, some more than you will ever know.

"Have fun and be goofy!" The photo above was the result. It was the last photo we took that day. Little did we know, that would be the last time we would see one another but your message and favorite quote remained with me:

"Be the change that you wish to see in the world".
–Mahatma Gandhi

Through your actions, you inspired me to live in color every day. You inspired other to spread happiness and positivity in your honor. This one is for you. Thank you. We love and miss you.

CONTENTS

ACKNOWLEDGMENTS

To the people who have given me tremendous inspiration, encouragement, and insight, I want to say thank you. You know who you are.

To my mother, there will never be enough words to express how grateful I am for you. I love you.

To those who assisted in my "failures", thank you.

"To live is the rarest thing in the world. Most people exist, that is all."

-Oscar Wilde

For Starters

Dom Mitchell

WHY THIS WAS WRITTEN

Wide eyed with the limitless world for the taking, sits us, as young kids at the edge of our seat ready to get started on our individual journeys of life. Our ceiling seemingly is non-existing and our worries lower than the ground we swing over, life is blissful. However, with many options of varying paths we can take in our life, the option of being happy and living our best life is one rarely heard and as we age, it is one that is thrown to the back of our minds as income takes priority in adulthood.

Society slashes our childhood dreams to pieces because they seem "unrealistic" for an adult to pursue. As we awake in the morning, we proceed to look at ourselves in the mirror but without acknowledgment of the kid inside of us all. Would the inner kid inside of us be proud of the person staring back at them in the mirror? Is that person living their best life or is that person simply going through the motions of life?

Joining the millions of walking dead every day, our happiness and life continues to be constricted by time frames other than our own. We work our asses off for jobs in which suck our souls dry and reward employees by allowing us to live a portion of our life away from work in the form of a few weeks vacation or retirement plan at the end of our lives when it is too late. Our dreams are put on hold without warning. What we want in life becomes the phrase: "One-day".

"One-day" transitions into "I wish I had" in what may seem like the blink of an eye. Years go by and life happens. Before we know it, here comes marriage, kids of our own, finances, timing, and whatever other excuses out of fear are used to justify us putting off our best life. If we allow things to snowball, they will and there will be no stopping it because at some point it will be too much. At that point, we get ourselves in such a hole it is hard to escape. The kid in us deserves to smile brightly again. We deserve to smile wholesomely with no regrets. We deserve to live a life we truly enjoy day in and day out. Throw away any excuses you may have and begin living in color. Celebrate your best life with the younger you and the person you will most certainly become in the future.

For those of us who feel as if who they are is simply not enough for every situation they may face. For those of us who feel their dreams have been muted by the rules someone else created or the expectations other than their own. For those of us whom may currently feel stuck in life and are in the process of finding their true self. For the people who wish to live life their way unapologetically. For those of us who crave to achieve their best life while improving their happiness and the happiness of others. This was written for you.

INTRODUCTION

Life is boring or so I had thought at the time. Seventy plus more years of this shit!? That's what I have to look forward to? No. No! This can't be right! There has to be more to life than this. Life cannot be meant to simply go to work, drink the weekend away, and repeat with hopes of getting somewhere someday. Someday… Imagine saying "one day if I work hard enough, I'll be able to live how I want". It deeply saddens me to partake in such thoughts. What if someday never came or better; what if someday was tomorrow?

You see, while you're growing up, your parents in particular and other people tell you how amazing life is. They speak highly of things you can do and let you know the world is at your fingertips if you're willing to stretch for it. They aren't wrong. You can truly accomplish your wildest dreams if you dared to dream but they are only speaking in terms of life up until you turn the sweet age of twenty-five. Well, the expectations of twenty-five anyway.

By the age of twenty-five, a person is expected to have gone to college, in the midst of starting a promising job, met your soul mates or seriously dating, and possibly create little bundles of joy or at least be thinking about it but is that really all there is to life? No one ever says what happens after college in terms of the month-to-month, the week-to-week, or hell, even the day-to-day. Only the milestones are mentioned but life isn't necessarily sparkles and fairy tales in between.

Truth be told, life can become quite mundane while we sit in the waiting room of life waiting for certain milestones to be birthed. We work hard to drink on the weekends, or weekdays depending on if you can function without alcohol or not. The problem lies in this: we party like everything is great, and for the most part it is but as Monday comes, the complaints roll in only for us to repeat the same actions for yet another week. Why is it this way? Where is the real fun? Where is the damn excitement!? When did it become acceptable for us to accept this way of life because this wasn't my dream life at 16 and damn sure isn't my dream now.

Eighteen to twenty-two, you go off to college and party it up. Making plenty of mistakes that don't seem to harm your current life much because you can chalk it up to being in college and all is forgiven. "I've been there! We all make mistake when we're young" is the typical response. Make your mistakes early, your parents tell you. It's supposed to be a clear path from here, earning the lucrative degree and nabbing that good job to boost your career; life will be easy. What if the biggest mistake we make during our life is not living life the way we want to?

What transpires if you don't obtain the status driven job or it is not as easy of a path as you were sold on OR god forbid, you don't go to college? Gasp! You might as well stop living! It's laid out for you, written in plain English at the beginning of the handbook of life and how to live yours. Oh wait, that's right, there is no handbook. Especially not one to tell you how to live your own life! If one were to be in existence, someone else would have written it and that doesn't seem right. How would they be able to write a handbook tailored specifically for your unique life when they are not you?

That was the question I began asking myself when I turned sixteen. I was seventeen when I began my "I don't give a fuck" career. If you didn't like my decisions or me, that was on you. I was going to live my life the way I wanted to regardless of what you thought or wanted me to do. I hadn't known it yet at the time but this notion ignited my first friendventory. It was pure bliss, to be quite honest. I wasn't living to impress anyone or doing things I did not enjoy anymore. I was simply living my life the way I wanted.

I was twenty when my mom noticed said career choice. She resisted the notion and her resistance further pushed my understanding that you simply cannot please everyone. Had I listened to her, my friends at the time would not have been supportive and had I took their advice, my mom sure as hell would have beat me into the previous week so I could relive her wrath one more time. No matter how hard I tried or what I did, there was displeasure from someone other than me.

Somewhere between twenty-one and twenty-three, I lost my job at IDGAF INC. I'm not entirely sure what took place but one day I woke up and was no longer employed by them. It could have been my longtime girlfriend at the time that didn't particularly care for that mindset or possibly it was a job that became too hard to keep up with. Quite possibly it was a mixture of both. The never-ending run-ins with the laws of an early adulthood relationship didn't gel well when it came to meeting the family. Nevertheless, my stance had softened. I began waiting on people to make a decision before making my own, I lived by others' rules, and I wanted to impress strangers before impressing myself but I was happy! Wasn't I?

Far from happiness, I was on an island of expectations by myself. Loneliness was my best friend even though people who cared for me surrounded me on a daily basis. I was at an age where my peers were graduating college and moving on with their life while I was stuck figuring mine out. I was in school at the time as well. Life looked great from an outsider's perspective but was it because it was what I wanted or was being in school what I was told I needed to do? The answer at the time was "absolutely" because I was told I needed to and the last time I checked, I didn't live by the rules of anyone else. The awakening of my true inner self erupted in a split second and the realization of my best life became crystal clear. The time to live my best life is now, not at a moment later.

I thought it over for months before pulling the trigger, going back and forth over the pros and cons of making changes in my life. The hesitation left me paralyzed, allowing fear to secrete in the folds of every thought and doubt to befriend itself with the excuses of fear. If I were going to do this, I needed a plan. So a plan is what I made. Photography is great but I wasn't trying to be the best studio photographer. In fact, the idea bored me. There was no excitement and the creativity seemed to have a ceiling to some degree. I switched my major and ultimately had to leave school because the major was not offered. Leaving school was the best choice for my happiness and me. I decided to go to a university to pursue another passion of mine, kinesiology, and English, but I certainly wanted and needed a break from the academic pursuit. My break lasted four long fulfilling years and consisted of getting a job in the field of study I was going for, getting experience, and living life while trying to make a living in the working world.

My break lasted longer than I expected but it was for the best. Learning all I could on my own and eventually getting to the highest point at the job, it was time to go after my dream. Failure was encouraged. Fear in which was not welcomed before now was my best friend. Mentally, I was prepared to progress and confident in my abilities to do whatever it took to get to the next step. The cursor winked as if it were a woman luring me down the hall to her room; four years later, I was back in school.

With a clear understanding of what I wanted out of school, unlike before, I was ready to take in the information presented. Mentally, I was nowhere near ready to take in the material in my last stint because I hadn't really known what I wanted to get out of the process and let outside distractions affect my life. This time around was divergent. This time, I was in school for me and no one else. Not because I was told I needed to and definitely not because it was expected of me.

Before my first day took place, my life at the time consisted of working, going home, working out a few days a week, and that was it. I lived too far from friends and family and was often too damn tired to muster up enough energy to put on pants. Once they were off, they were off. Truth be told, I was borderline depressed because there simply was no one around who seemed to understand me. I hadn't seen much of my family and my engagement was on the rocks.

Life became tough at precisely the right moment. Life becoming tough usually provides the best outcomes, however, it became apparent something was wrong with me. I had been experiencing unusual exhaustion, head fog, memory loss, irritable outbursts, and to top it off, an irritable bowel. I later found my energy was being sapped faster than a smartphone running ten applications because of the food I was eating. I had been killing myself and didn't know it. Eating well and moving well became a top priority in my life especially considering the fact school was only months away; I needed to be on top of my game, mentally and physically. I focused on transitioning my eating habits to a more sustainable way of eating and rebooting my metabolism in order to be happier and healthier. This was the first step in turning my life around.

The months during the summer prior to the fall quarter beginning, I began reading more, ultimately sparking this journey towards achieving my best life. My engagement was over and instead of wallowing around like a piece of clothing left over from a one night stand, I decided to kick start my learning through reading. Book after book, page after page, I became more inclined to living a life unfamiliar to my previous understanding. It turned out I was right, after all, life was not supposed to be as boring as it was previously, I simply did not understand nor appreciate the true beauty of life.

Life took an unpredictable turn for the best, creating a perspective of love, selflessness, and realization of a larger purpose. As blood rushed from my head, I laid there on a sidewalk with an open wound the size of a baseball revealing everything a person should not be able to see. That's a bit disgusting, isn't it? That's how I felt about my life before deciding to achieve my best life: disgusting. Going to the gym, going to work, having a rare weekend on the town, and repeating that routine week after week? What the fuck is that! Excuse my

French but that is certainly not a proper representation of who I am. That is not my life and certainly not the life that screams I'm giving my effort, wouldn't you agree?

I needed to be a great role model not only for my family but also for the youth who needs someone to look up to and even more so, a role model to my younger self for I know how much I needed to hear this while I was growing up.

With age comes the appreciation of the beauty in the process of life. Finding the beauty in learning all you possibly can. Finding the beauty in oneself and loving you for who you truly are. Finding the beauty in eating well, moving well, reading more, and traveling often. When you're young, the beauty is in the fun of life. You feel invincible! However, as you progress in age, the beauty is in the process of life. You appreciate the feeling of vulnerability and learn to enrich life through a variety of avenues. If you can find the beauty early, your best life is around the corner.

Grab a drink because we're making a toast: From this day forward, we live in color; here's to achieving our best life! Salud!

1

THERE ARE NO RULES

"Be the change that you wish to see in the world"

–Mahatma Gandhi

There I was, standing in the midst of everyone's expectations except my own of what I should be and what I should do with my life with guarantees it will make me happier, also providing the best life. They say: Follow this rule and you'll get this result, never do this or it will end like this, you have to do it this way, you need to do it that way... They are all opinions, plain and simple.

To become happier, you should first acknowledge and wholesomely understand this one simple rule, a rule in which I wish I had known sooner in life and that is: there are no rules in life except for those that we create by attempting to live our best life. If life were as easy as we are told, it being almost black & white with no gray area, the rules would never change. Life needs color. It needs drama and excitement almost as much as a reality television show. Instead of conforming to old rules, make your own. Choose to live in color and create your best life.

With neither a right nor a wrong way to live a happy and fulfilled life, there certainly is not a handbook on life that guarantees anything if you follow step x and end with step y. If such a thing existed, everyone would have a copy and you wouldn't be reading this. There are only suggestions and biased opinions. Being told to do something a certain way because others have also done it in a similar fashion, is not living your best life.

To have a standard, someone had to create the said standard. The standard did not become the standard out of thin air. Standards and rules are set and made by the person attempting to create their best life. Live your life your way and create your own standard. Why should you not be allowed to create your own? Through trials and tribulations, ultimately you are the only one who can decide if something works in life or does not work. With that being said, what works for one person, may not work for another. Allow me to offer a perspective.

What is the definition of perfection? It mostly depends on whom you ask. A better question would be, what is your definition of perfection? Once you can clearly define your definition of perfection, the beginning attempt at creating your best life will begin. Perfection is a perception that lies within true happiness of the beholder. If we were taught what perfection is supposed to look like, it can also be forgotten and relearned to mirror how we want it to look like. In life, only we can define what is perfect and what is not based on personal life experiences, desires, wants, and needs. Again, what may be perfect for one may not be perfect for another. The mind of those who are happy truly creates their own version of perfection from within. I am not saying you need to be happy in order to create perfection but it is difficult to create it otherwise. I have never encountered a person in a state of sadness or in any state besides happy, that concluded they were living their best life.

The definition of happiness can also vary depending on the person who is being asked. Some value materialistic possessions over experiences and some value experiences over materialistic possessions. Which person is happier? There is no clear answer because an outside person cannot know what truly makes another person happy. We can only focus on our personal happiness and how we can repeatedly create our own. Finding true happiness is a process that will take time to achieve. Furthermore, it is a process that will result in us doing things beyond our imagination and comfort zone.

Since deciding to live my best life, I've done things and have seen things that still baffle me till this day; some of which will never touch the ears of my mother or grandparents. Meeting a variety of new life and creating friendships that otherwise would not have been created if I continued to live a life with rules created by others, has been the best part of this journey. Stepping out of my comfort zone and realizing I'm in full control of my life, lead to events that created unpredictable excitement, random robust laughter, and memories that will last past my lifetime. Happiness, to me, comes from creating excitement within life and having balance throughout. How would you define happiness?

As the old saying goes, "you cannot buy happiness". Truth be told, the saying holds some merit. While we can't buy our way to being happy, we surely can buy it temporarily. How many of us have bought something and have been completely happy after? I know I have. However, that happiness is temporary. When I mention buying happiness temporarily, I'm speaking in terms of buying something small to create happy memories that can't be replaced. Creating residual happiness. This could mean going out to your local store, purchasing water balloons and a couple of squirt guns, inviting people to bring their own and have an all out water fight in the park. It might not cost much money and may not seem like much compared to buying yourself a new closet of clothes but the memories of laughter and fun with friends will last forever.

Like a car, a brand new one is shiny and nice at first but eventually, you become used to it and it no longer holds that "new" feeling; fulfilling temporary happiness. However, memories of happiness can never get old. They can always be replayed but never repeated in the same fashion, creating residual happiness. Life is at its best when we create residual happiness and ultimately decide what a happy life looks like to us.

Think of your life as a company. Once a company starts, they need policies and regulations. Who creates said policies and regulations? Typically, the owner creates them with input from outside sources as suggestions. Ultimately, the owner has the final say on what is done and what is not. The policies get updated as time progresses and methods are tested, only changing them when doing things a certain way, generate certain results or lack thereof. Determining what works best and what does not, eliminating what did not work and continuing to move forward. You are the owner of your life. Find what works best for you and eliminate what does not. Striving to live our best life depends on this strategy.

Sure, there are best practices and examples of happy and successful lives but with that being said, we also are the only ones who may define what is and what is not considered a happy and successful life. Remember, those who deviated from the standard and created their own rules created the new standard. Those who are not afraid to try, often make the rules.

When I say there are no rules in life, it's a challenge and a reminder. It's a challenge to not only myself but to everyone who reads this book. It's a challenge to our current state of mind and actions we partake in our daily lives. A reminder that we have complete control over our lives if we leap from our fears and simply give effort. Those who do not try will forever live in ignorance and those who do try, success or failure, will reap the benefits of attempting to live a better life. Therefore, I challenge myself and everyone else to give our best effort every second possible. Even if something is fearful to the point of crapping our pants, we must try. You will only begin to achieve your best life, once you decide to break the rules by living a life creating your own. Our happiness relies on our willingness to create our own rules and attempts to live our best life. At what point will you start living for yourself? Make it tomorrow.

2

FIXED MINDSET

When you think of the phrase "fixed mindset", what comes to mind? Personally, it allows my thoughts to gravitate towards a preconceived notion that cannot and will not be changed. Consequently, the term also carries a tone in which progress seems to be deterred from transpiring. At some point in life, every person falls into a fixed mindset. Whether it is consciously or subconsciously, it needs to be broken for you to reach your life's max potential. The old saying of "if it's not broken, don't fix it", does not apply here. If we don't break this mindset, how will we know if it was truly working or not? Break it and do not look back.

To create your best life, live yours within a growth mindset. The word growth embeds a powerfully positive tone. Simply saying the word makes you feel more at ease and empowered. We have two options after entering a fixed mindset. Option A is to stay within said mindset and continue life as is. There is nothing wrong with this mindset but my guess is you have this book in your hands because it is not the option you would like to live. Option B is to transition into a growth mindset. This does not come easily but is the most beneficial to living your best life. Rome was not built in a day and neither will an amazingly happy and fulfilled life. The goal is not to forget what made you, you, but to use your life experiences to learn from your mistakes, distance yourself from those mistakes by gaining the courage to try again, and using your mindset to achieve what seemed to be out of reach previously.

The beginning step in ending a fixed mindset to enter a growth mindset comes by way of reminding and challenging us to live a life with "no rules". We also have to in a way, forget the things we previously knew. A majority of our best lives consists of us doing the things we love and all of us, or a large majority of us, have thought about it at one point or another; quitting your day job to pursue something you truly love. That's saying if what you're doing is not fulfilling your happiness at this point of course. Doing something you love and not worrying about which particular day it is because every day is a new journey seems to be a better option than complaining about a job, which kills your soul five days out of the week.

That is truly the dream but not many live it. I too came to the realization my soul was being sucked dry by a job that held absolutely no meaning to my life or anyone else's. Similar to many others, I was going through the daily motions and focusing on things in which we feel are important at the moment but turn out to be a distraction more than anything; only to look up one day to realize time has flown by with having next to nothing to show for it. Not being happy in what you're doing carries over into many aspects of your life and plays a vital role in the longevity of your life. Once I noticed this pattern, the power of life began to shift more favorably. Personally, there is a lengthy list of goals and interests I plan to accomplish and explore over the duration of my life, however, at the time, I looked up and noticed I wasn't doing anything close to what I actually wanted to be doing. There was something atrociously wrong with that image and my younger self would be disappointed in me if he were told this was the life he'd be living.

The beginning of anything new and unfamiliar can be the most daunting part of the process. Especially as long as what we love is surrounded by the words "hard" or "impossible". Of course, whenever we listen to that of what we previously knew, things will definitely be hard or impossible but to create your best life, you must be willing to find a new way of doing things. Remember, the word fixed equates to stagnation while the word growth elicits advancement. Ask questions but find a new answer, an answer that brings a smile to your soul and younger self. The same people who will tell you you're crazy are the same people who will wonder how you did it. Starting is the largest step and once you overcome it, you can handle anything that may come your way.

As overwhelming as it may seem, you will undoubtedly have some questions to start out. Such as how to start and where to start. This is the point in which most people quit because either they spend too much time trying to find the perfect answer or take so much time to find the perfect answer they psych themselves out of starting. In order to achieve your best life, you need to in a sense, quit what you've been doing for your entire life and start completely fresh. Nonetheless, doing so will rid you of a fixed mindset, adopting a growth mindset in return. Erasing your previous knowledge of how to do things and becoming open to learning or creating distinct ways of living is not an easy task. It's about as tough to do as getting up at 4 AM during the winter. However, it is of necessity to work hard and overcome the thoughts of quitting when the results aren't as swift as you'd like or had hoped for. There are many paths to take in life but when you crave to achieve your best life, there are always questions and doubts but should you let them stop you? Your actions are as critical as your response.

Invest

To truly change, investing in yourself before anything or anyone else separates you from the pack. Starting out, identify everything you may need in order to achieve your desired results and make a list of it. Please do yourself the favor and do your homework! Research and take your time deciding what you need. The keyword here is: need, not want. If it takes a month or longer to compile everything, so be it but get started sooner rather than later and put your efforts and energy towards the most important person in your life; you. Remember, you're the owner in your life. Invest in your life today for your best life tomorrow. If that means getting your hair cut every week to spark positive feelings because it makes you feel better, so be it. If you feel you need a better (insert item here) to accomplish the goal, add it. Whatever it is, if you truly feel like it will help you reach the next step, do it; invest. The goal here is not to find material things that we want but to identify what we need to progress not only ourselves but our happiness as well.

Write it down

Since you're listing things, you're going to need a

notebook or something to take notes on. I recommend something small because it is easy to carry around to keep as a reminder throughout the day. Carrying something around to jot down ideas helped me tremendously and continues to do so. You may have these great ideas or moments of break through and hours later won't be able to remember your exact train of thought. This is where a small journal comes in handy. Take the time to whip it out and write down your thoughts or anything that will make you remember that train of thought. Different people take different notes or have different ways of remembering things so this is only a suggestion. Find what works best for you.

Take it easy on yourself

It is not a race and there is no perfect way to do this. Give yourself plenty of time and plenty of encouragement. I know I can be a bit hard on myself and other people can as well but, in order to progress, appreciation of how far you've come is key to move past any current limitations. Take a moment to look back at where you've started and focus on the positive things that have come since that point in time. We often want instant gratification but understand that it may take days, weeks, months, or even years for things to get going. Do a little each day and stay focused. You are your worst critic they say but in the interest of achieving your best, you need to be your best supporter.

Understand and accept the process

Everything you do will not be perfect, including the process of transitioning into a growth mindset. Even if you feel like you have the best of the best, in a month or in a year, you'll want to change it in order to continue your progress. That is what your best life is about; continuous improvement. This is the process. It does not matter how you start but starting is the first step. Your beginning will look nothing like your end or even your middle. This is coming from a self-proclaimed perfectionist; let it go. It will be fine.

The small details you'll incur along the way, most people probably won't notice or won't bother to care to notice. Change is difficult. If you're a full-time employee at Perfectionist INC, please terminate employment immediately. Let things go and understand while we may not be able to see the future, things do happen for a reason. Trust in yourself and the journey you will be embarking on.

Choose wisely

Your decisions you make in your life from here on out need to be chosen wisely with a hint of "what do you have to lose?" From the language we use and surround ourselves with to the people, we choose to spend our time around and the language they use will be important in your creation. Great examples here are students. If you're a student and you'd like to achieve the coveted A grade, would you sit around the kids who are failing or barely getting by? No, you'd want to sit around the kids who are getting A's as well because they will rub off on you or at the very least, you'll end up getting some solid help. There is no cheating in this case.

Now, I know it's difficult to quit old relationships but if those relationships are not helping you progress or the language being used isn't stimulating your mind, why continue to allow yourself to be in that environment? I'm not saying drop your friends but I am advising you to expand your connections. Meet other people who are like-minded and challenge yourself to push past your initial thoughts into greater possibilities. Allow yourself to enter a growth atmosphere and you will reap the benefits.

Once you begin your transition, ask yourself two questions:

1) Why not you? After answering this question, ask yourself the following:
2) What is there to lose?

There is no reason a particular dream or goal of yours cannot be done by you and when you push aside excuses, fear, and uncalled for doubt, there is also nothing to lose. Whatever it is you feel like you can lose, 90 percent of the time it can be reversed. Often times the things we are most fearful of, never happen, ultimately leaving us paralyzed with no attempt to show for it. A failed attempt is only one in which was never attempted.

Compare life to that of an arrow in the hands of an archer. An arrow that is not released either stays in the same place or goes backward and returns to its original starting point with no progress being made. From the previous chapter, you know our happiness begins when we attempt to create our own rules and live our best life, the key word being: attempt. To do so, we need to release our fears. Aim your arrow, pull it back, breathe, and release. The distance and accuracy of the arrow will ultimately be decided by how much effort and practice you put forth.

Change is hard to swallow for most. We are used to seeing something and desire consistency. However, life can and will never be consistent because life itself is in a growth mindset. Be willing to adapt and mirror the same mindset as life. Attempt to live your best life by creating your own rules and shifting into a growth mindset. Are you crazy or are have you simply had enough of living life shaped by the standards of others?

3

ACTIONS BEGET FEELINGS

"The difference between who you are and who you want to be is what you do."
—Bill Phillips

Have you ever met someone with the energy of a new puppy, an attitude so positive it made your negative thoughts regurgitate, and a happiness which made you smile, that you had no choice but to succumb to it yourself? Happiness and positivity are extremely contagious! The manner in which we act has a tremendous impact on our mood whether we realize it at the time or not. Acting in a happy manner rather than a negative manner ignites positive feelings. Who doesn't want to become happier while achieving their best life? I've never met someone who has said: "I don't need any more happiness in my life" and if they did, they were probably being dishonest with themselves. The way the world stands right now, there is an abundance of hate and negativity swirling around imitating a tornado. Don't add to it. Rather, spread those contagious traits and change someone's day. Better yet, change your own day. You can't control anyone else but you have full control over yourself. When you act as if you feel good, you begin to feel good. When you feel good, you do good and when you do good, you feel good.

I personally wanted to have more energy throughout my days. However, I noticed there would be things I would let get in the way of me achieving the said goal; sitting in traffic, not getting enough sleep at night, not eating enough food throughout the day, people using negative language, etc. Life has come to a crossroad where now, I want to be the contagious person in the room in the most positive way possible. Acting how I wanted to feel in order to diminish a negative feeling from spreading like wildfire and spread the energy of happiness instead. For example, if I'm tired and moving sluggishly, I'll act more energetic by listening to music and dancing. It's a false energy but sometimes you have to fake it to make it. This is the next step in creating your best life. Being able to identify how you're feeling and counteract a negative feeling with a positive action is a continuation of your growth.

Achieving your best life means to be able to control your actions and enhance the positive feelings of others, creating a domino effect. The term "pay it forward" can be an adopted mindset we take on here. Performing a good deed for someone else makes the other person feel good and makes you feel good as well. Generally, your positive actions will spark another person to do the same and so on. Our actions drive our energy. If we act negatively, we achieve negative results. While creating your best life, there is no room for negative actions or results. The words "create" and "best" are two terms, whether alone or combined, embrace progress. You cannot create nor get the best results without acting in a positive manner. Not only acting in a positive manner but spreading happiness and positivity to anyone who may come in your presence. Your best life includes being selfless enough to help others achieve theirs as well.

Karma is one hell of a woman. She is the most vengeful person you will ever encounter but also the most endearing and generous woman you will ever come across. When we allow negative actions to determine our feelings and use those negatives feelings to determine our actions, karma rears her ugly vengeful head to remind you of what you have done. However, when we allow the opposite to occur, karma rewards us beautifully. It may be in different forms such as a new opportunity in life or a promotion but regardless of what the generous reward may be, it always feels amazing when something good happens to us. We are only rewarded positively when we act positively.

In no way should you disregard or discredit negative emotions. This is the real world after all and we cannot be happy every single second of the day. We are only human but we can try our best to be a fortress of solitude to give ourselves the highest chance to succeed at achieving our best life. Other emotions in life are certainly validated. As mentioned before, while we can only control ourselves, at times an outside source can spark an emotional change or hell, some days we are simply not having our best days. Nevertheless, embrace those emotions and accept them for what they are. Having enough control over yourself to notice those emotions and counter them with a positive action, takes more strength than allowing those emotions to dictate or decide the outcome of your day. Become mindful enough to recognize when you're not at your best. Being mindful is something I'll touch on in later chapters but it is important to note what words or actions brought about certain emotions in order to prevent them in the future or repeat them if they bring about positive emotions.

The journey of achieving my best life took a Usain Bolt like jolt when I decided I'm going to focus on smiling, laughing, and having more fun in life. Negativity would not be allowed around my fortress. As impossible as that sounded at the time, it was the mere decision to give the effort to eliminate things I felt were a threat to my best life, which made it possible. I should say for clarification, it is not perfect but I try my best to not let negativity affect me, and that in itself drove me towards my best life along with creating my own rules, giving effort, transitioning to a growth mindset, and acting in accordance to how I wanted to feel. I want my energy to positively affect others and spread like wildfire. The real change we desire comes from within ourselves. Focus your energy to control the things you can control and have fun while doing so, others will take notice and want to join along.

4

BE "YOU"

"We are who we are depending on the situation that we are in."
–Kobe Bryant

"You should know you're beautiful just the way you are
And you don't have to change a thing, the world could change its heart"
-Alessia Cara

"More than simply a positive mood, happiness is a state of well-being that encompasses living a good life—that is, with a sense of meaning and deep satisfaction. Research shows that happiness is not the result of bouncing from one joy to the next; achieving happiness typically involves times of considerable discomfort."
-Psychology Today

Living your best life holds an entirely different meaning depending on the person you ask but yields the best answers from those who are happy with being themselves. Being yourself is the toughest part in achieving your best life but is the most important. To be yourself, you first must be happy with who you are, love you are, understand who you were, and be open to who you will become. In order to be happy and love the person you are, you must not be afraid to be yourself every second of the days that lie ahead. This will require you to break the social norms at times. Be the "you" you are when you're alone because that's the real unfiltered you, the "you" that deserves to be seen. It will be tough at first but the best things in life are also the toughest to obtain. A life of acceptance while wearing a mask of another is not your best life; it is someone else's. Force people to accept who you are by being nothing short of your true self whenever you can. Your best life will only be obtained by your willingness to go against expectations of who you should be and be the person you want to be.

A path untraveled is a path unknown.

While it may seem obvious to some that achieving your best life includes being yourself, not everyone will come to this conclusion on their own or may think they currently know themselves wholeheartedly. Fortunately, none of us will ever know who we truly are if we're giving our max effort towards achieving our best life. I say fortunately because not knowing who we fully are would mean we are always growing and putting forth effort in developing ourselves further in life; never settling for what we know and always pushing ourselves to our individual limits.

We may get close to knowing who we are while on our journey to our best life but since we are aiming for the best, we are constantly trying new things and creating new experiences to enjoy. You cannot possibly know if you like something or dislike something until you try it. There are a ton of things to do in this wonderful world and we have nothing but time to do them all or at least attempt to do most of them. Become more of yourself by finding what it is you do or do not like to do and create experiences that will last a lifetime.

This step may bring about some backlash from those around you. By being your true self it may seem as if you changed but in reality, you are just being the real "you". Any time another person acts in a way someone else does not agree with, that person is blistered with "you've changed" comments. If this happens, understand others' frustration. They are used to a certain "you" and if you recall in previous chapters, we know people dislike change and prefer consistency. Achieving your best life means you cannot please everyone in the process. We all want to be liked but that simply is an impossible feat. Your actions will please some and in the same instance, will displease others. No matter what you do, someone is either going to agree with your decisions or disagree with them. There will not be unanimous agreement across the board. Base your decisions solely on what will truly make you happy and what you want. Suggestions are nice but ultimately, you have to live with any decisions you make.

I wish I had learned this step sooner in my journey but it is better to learn when you are ready to fully understand the lesson at hand than to learn when you aren't willing to change. While working in the fitness industry, a coworker and I were having a conversation and he says, "I say what I want because people are going to make up in their minds whether or not they like you regardless of what you do or say" and this resonated with me deeply. We are not promised tomorrow so to live a life holding back words and actions in which represent us, truly would be a life unfulfilled. If someone wants to like you, they will like you but if someone does not want to like you, they will find any and every excuse to dislike you. It is important to say and do the things we want because our best life also contains absolute no regrets. What do you have to lose?

Say yes to life when you normally would say no but only say yes to things you truly want to do. You don't know if you like something until you try it. I recommend staying far away from drugs but hey if that is something you want to do and you feel that is the path to your best life, who am I to tell you otherwise? This is your best life, not mine. With that being said, the movie "Yes Man" starring Jim Carey embeds a strong message; saying yes to life creates moments that would otherwise be missed but understanding saying yes only should come as a result of the individual's true desires.

Do you truly like something or do you like it because you have been taught to enjoy it? As children, we enjoy a variety of things as we are learning how to navigate through life. However, we are often met by the expectations of society and are taught we should like certain things based off of our gender. Men should like and do things more of masculine nature and women should like and do things of feminine nature.

Ridiculed if we deviate from social norms, it prevents us from truly being ourselves. Men are often being peppered with names such as "bitch", "pussy", and "fag" eluding they are weak and sensitive. Women are ousted by their female peers if she seems to be too much of "one of the boys" and is deemed not one of the group. You cannot be afraid to be you. Rather than becoming upset by the lack of acceptance, realize those who live in the shadows of what others want and are anything short of being their true self, are not achieving their best life.

As adults, we are still told what we should or should

not do and sometimes we even agree to do things when we know we do not like them. For example, going out to the bar. I personally do not like to go to the bar much because to me, it's a waste of money and time. I'd much rather use the $10-$30 towards a trip, clothes, good memories, concert, etc. At times I'll accept the invite and go out anyway. I do not like being the guy who always says no so on occasion I will say yes in order to keep friendships alive. Now don't get me wrong, hanging out with friends is great! However, paying for over priced liquor and going to a bar or a club to socialize is just not my cup of whiskey. I'd much rather prefer to have friends over while preparing a large meal and discuss our goals or ambitions as the time becomes a faint remembrance in our minds. The lesson here is it is ok to accept an invitation if you don't like something but accept with an acknowledgment that even though you do not particularly enjoy the event, the choice to attend is solely yours.

This is a great time to be a bit selfish in your life. A person may be upset with your choices but will have no reason other than to respect the fact you're aiming towards a better you and your best life. Being you includes doing the things you like to do regardless if someone agrees or disagrees. If you don't feel comfortable at first, it is important to remember a moment is only that; a small moment in time which will quickly pass over.

Truth be told and as surprised as you may be to hear this but no one really cares about the things you're doing. They don't! Most people are paying more attention to what they have going on in their life. Sure, they may take notice to you for a moment but once that moment passes, it's back to them.

We might as well be ourselves as well as we can with

the moments we have. Every person on this planet is insecure in some way or another. You are no different. To be yourself, you first must be happy with who you are, love you are, understand who you were, and be open to who you will become. Confidently break out of who you are today to become the "you" you are tomorrow.

"Find out who you are and do it on purpose."
–Dolly Parton

5

FRIENDVENTORY

"You are the company you keep"
-Proverbs 13:20

"So what I wanna talk about tonight is, why are your
friends so annoying? It doesn't make any sense--these are
the people you have PICKED to be with! You like these
people and yet everything that they do--you're never
going to the right restaurant!"
–Jerry Seinfeld

The people in whom we surround ourselves with will
ultimately play a large role in our desired objective. You
are the owner in your life and as the owner; you will need
to perform a full friendventory of your current
relationships. What exactly is a friendventory? And why is
it that we need to do one? Fantastic question. A
friendventory, if you haven't already guessed is an
inventory of our friends. Why do we need to do one?
Well, we'll get to that in a second. This may sound silly
but by doing an inventory of our friends, we can further
understand not only ourselves but also our future.
Strongly focusing on our best life and what types of
relationships we want. Although it may sound selfish, our
happiness should always be a top priority. We want

friends who can keep us spiritually connected, elevate us, and grow with us constantly.

Unfortunately, we cannot do all of life's activities with every person. That's the honest truth and there's nothing wrong with that! It's a good idea to have a culmination of friends who fit into the individual goals and ambitions we have in life, whether that may be current goals or future ones. There should always be someone in our corner who further enhances who we are and vice versa. After all, friendships are a two-way street.

If we want to know where we will be in five years, take a look at the people we have surrounded ourselves with and notice what they are doing with their life. Does their drive and ambition match yours? Are they strong in an area that you are weak? Do your friends also wish to achieve their best life? If so, wonderful! If not, you may need to make some changes. If our friends are going places in life and creating opportunities for themselves, their drive will rub off on us and in return, should enhance our goals or at the very least, make us want to level up to keep up with them. This is a huge reason why we need to do a friendventory.

In order to progress, you need the correct like-minded people around you. A prime example of this comes from sports. Have you ever witnessed an athlete who was dominating the rest of the competition but when entering the professional level, their performance diminished? Or have you seen a younger kid playing with the adults because playing with kids their age simply is not challenging enough? This happens for a few reasons.

One of the reasons stems from the truthful fact that the competition is only being dominated because the opposing star athlete is playing against a level of talent in which will never reach the professional level. When this is the case, once the star athlete goes professional, the competition is stiffer and up to par, raising the level of difficulty to perform at such a high level and thus creating the drop in production. Some people can adapt and continue success and some people simply cannot keep up. Those who cannot adapt are considered a "bust". The athletes who adapt, typically have a strong support system in place in forms of team staff and veteran players to mentor them as well as a willingness to put forth the effort needed.

This should be the case with your relationships. Consider yourself a star athlete entering the professional level. The professional level represents your best life. Achieving it alone can be done but it is more difficult and also less joyful. Surround yourself with those who can assist you by playing ball with those who are ahead of you to learn and progress yourself further. Choose wisely because the right team will yield your desired results.

Too often, we hang onto relationships that are not beneficial to our best lives or us as an individual anymore. Old friendships are understandably hard to let go. However, some old friendships may still exist solely for the purpose of our comfort zone. Building new friendships takes effort as we grow with age and quite frankly, can be a bit uncomfortable at times. How will you know your full potential if you never allow yourself to build your network outside of the current relationships that exist in your life?

If an old friendship entails negative language or consists of doing things in which don't truly make you happy, is it benefiting your best life? These are tough questions to ask but are necessary for your development. Being brutally honest and unbiased in this step will take some time because when feelings are involved, it is never easy to cut ties. If you do have to sever ties but do not wish to do so completely, simply begin to become busy when invited out and offer to catch up down the line over food or a drink.

Achieving our best life can be a cruel battlefield like process. There will be casualties, enemies, and alliances built along the way in your growth. Stay on the progressive path by constantly performing and reevaluating your friendventory. Keep in mind you should almost always do things that are beneficial to you and your time. Your time is valuable and you should treat it as if it is gold. Not everyone is deserving of your time and energy. You have the final say in who will be apart of your journey and what you choose to do while on said journey.

Make Categories

Making categories allows us to put our interests/passions/goals into an organized list or chart. The categories also allow us to physically see the slots to do a side-by-side comparison. It is always a good idea to create a "balance" category for the friends who are well rounded and like-minded. Also, create a "just fun" category because sometimes we simply want to have fun and we all have that one friend who knows how to have a good time. It is ok to take a night off and let loose.

Create a list

We'll use this list to write down all of our friends or acquaintances and the type of friends we want to have in our life. For example, if we desire more friends who are into photography, jot it down but write down the relationships you want to have as the last step after your current relationships have been written. Deal with the current friends that are in your lives right now because they are the most important. They already physically exist. Your list should consist of close friends first followed by secondary friends, acquaintances, and ending with relationships we do not currently have but desire.

Slot it

As a final step, all that's left to do is insert your relationships into the categories you have created. Once you have, you can compare the areas that you currently have filled versus the areas you need or want to fill voids in.

This may seem weird to some and can be seen as a game to most but when it comes to our future and our happiness, it is never a game. The truth can hurt and us being honest about whom we keep around us in our lives can be difficult but it is necessary. Some relationships are toxic and some are beneficial. With none of us knowing our timetable for life, it's too short to live it unhappy and unprogressive.

Whether we want to admit it or not, all relationships have an expiration date. Some relationships may expire quickly and some may expire when we expire. We have no way of knowing when they will expire but people come into our lives for a reason. While they are here, appreciate them for everything the relationship is.

The quality in which we live our lives matters tremendously in our end goal and can inspire others to value the quality of their life as well. You have full control in obtaining what you want out of life. Break the rules and live your best life by creating your own, trying your best, shifting into a growth mindset, spreading happiness and positivity, being your true self, and paying attention to the company you keep.

6

CONTEMPLATE LIFE

"Many people die at twenty-five and aren't buried until
they are seventy-five."
–Benjamin Franklin

We take life for granted. Every single person has, at
some point in time, taken for granted how lucky he or she
has it. The belief of there will be a tomorrow, allows us to
put things off and leave words unsaid. To achieve our
best life, we must slow ourselves down to appreciate life
as it is. One summer morning in the year 2016, I had a
breakdown. At the time, I was working out in my
apartment and on the television was a sports debate
show. While I cannot recall exactly what was said to spark
the breakdown, it was the emotion and thoughts the
debate evoked that is of importance here. I began to think
about the circumstances of death and what it would mean
to others around me.

While death frightened me, the idea of leaving words
unsaid, having regrets of not living my best life, losing the
ability to see those who I love, and not inspiring others'
lives frightened me more so than actual death itself. For
all I had known, my next drive to work could have been
my last. A million questions ran through my head within
minutes. Do they know I love them? Will anyone

remember me? Why didn't I do this when I had the chance? Why didn't I eat that burrito? This was not the life I was meant to lead. My best life was not being lived and that reality hit harder than a wrecking ball knocking down cement. It was time for a change. I needed to curtail going through the everyday motions and instead, slow down in order to appreciate what was in front of me. From that day forward, I decided to appreciate all things in life, leave nothing unsaid no matter how uncomfortable it made me, and live my way to achieve my best life.

There were days where I would drive and could not remember how I got from point A to point B. That was a serious and scary problem! How could I have driven for 30 minutes and not remember a single thing? It had become such a routine that my mind blanked out part of the day because there was no new information worth recording, or so I had thought. I'm sure some who will read this may resonate with this feeling or event. Making a conscious effort to remember small details on my drives, say them out loud as they were happening, and repeating them at the end of the day ignited my brain to begin to take note of small details in which separated the moments in my everyday activities. No two moments can or will ever be the same.

Have you ever been doing something or have been at an event and after it is over, can't remember it in detail a week later? I'm sure we all have. We live fast and forget to take a moment to truly appreciate an experience for what it is. I know I'm guilty of this, the assumption is tomorrow will be for certain and for the most part it is unless you're living like a wild child, jumping off of buildings for social media. With that being said, how are we to know when our time is up?

We eat as if another meal is coming when, for all we know (and god forbid), it could be our last. The burger you scarfed down in minutes may be something a person does not get to experience in his or her life and yet, you can get a burger whenever you please. As hard as it is to believe, there are people who do not get the opportunities we have and some, unfortunately, do not get to see tomorrow. Take your time chewing, savor the delicate flavors of which some do not have the same opportunity to taste, tell people you love them when you feel it, be in the moment, and realize you are where you're supposed to be at that very moment.

Become further present and mindful while living in each moment. While being present and being mindful essentially have the same meaning, each can be explained differently. Being mindful in this instance calls for paying attention to detail; how things feel by touch, how your body feels when you do certain tasks or movements, how things smell, etc. The saying, "you don't appreciate things until they are gone" is absolutely correct in every sense. Your best life cannot afford to wait for the unfortunate to take place. Appreciate what you have and those who around you while they are here before they are gone. Make the most of every situation by creating memories and excitement rather than living in the past or entertaining things in which you won't remember in ten years.

As humans we have the best and worst curse known to our kind; we are born to die. At some point in time, we will not be able to grace the ground in which we walk on daily with our presence. While we are here, we have the amazing opportunity to leave a mark that may last multiple lifetimes. You can literally do anything you want in life (please refer to chapter one for a review). The word death is used not to scare you but to make you understand the opportunity of life is a gift. How you live your life should be nothing short of your best. Again, the best can only to be defined by you.

Life is similar to traffic on a one-way highway. Each driver veers onto the highway from different ramps, at different times, and different locations, however, we are all driving in the same direction; albeit each driver has their own agenda. With a variety of cars on the road, in the end, every driver gets to his or her destination one way or the other. Some drivers are more anxious than others, some listen to music while others listen to talk radio, some enjoy the drive and some do not, some drive with one hand and others with two. Regardless of how we drive or what we do while we drive, there is not a wrong or right way to operate the vehicle. There are obvious rules in place to ensure we get to our destination in one piece and make it as safe as possible for others such as; driving lanes, speed limits, signs, and emergency exits. Understandably, the rules are in place because otherwise there would be complete chaos. Drivers who speed and drive recklessly, want to beat the traffic and make it to their destination as quickly as possible with no regard for other cars on the same highway. There are drivers who enjoy the scenery along the way. There are drivers whom will pull over for a break or to simply take in the sights. There are the drivers who are generous to let others in front of them because they want the flow of traffic to run smoothly. As you contemplate life and learn to appreciate the drive, ask yourself, what type of driver are you currently? And what type of driver would you like to be?

7

AIM HIGHER: DO YOU HAVE THE COURAGE?

"You have to be maniacal about living your best life"

It's halftime. You're down 30. It's not the time to panic. The only way to get out of this deficit and win is to chip away at the lead and to be determined. Stick to the plan and play your game. It has gotten you this far, trust it will help you win.

Let's discuss having courage. Courage is the ability to do something that frightens us but also having the ability to remain strong in the face of adversity. The process of achieving your best life will take the utmost courage. Period. This is purely an uncomfortable endeavor in which will change us forever. Courage is for the strong. Courage is for the determined. Courage is for those who are hell bent on living freely and being happy. Living your best life is not for the faint-hearted but is for those who are not afraid to shoot for their wildest dreams. Do you have enough courage to aim as high as possible?

Your answer lies within your actions. If you have been making progress through following the previous chapters, congratulations, you're on the right track to achieving your best life. If not, that's ok, this isn't a race and everyone sets his or her own pace; this also is not a step-by-step handbook. Hesitation can be a natural reaction here. We know hesitation is a place where doubts and fears go to wreak havoc on our motor systems, making it difficult to move as if we are in a straitjacket. This is a common occurrence when stepping onto unfamiliar grounds; it gets increasingly strenuous to end hesitations once it sets in. In terms of breaking into our best life, we will make more progress by acting first and asking questions second.

The excuse or fear of not being good enough is hesitation at its finest. Instead of having the courage to go straight for your target, you hesitate, allowing a multitude of excuses and fears to set in to talk you out of aiming high. You are absolutely good enough and never let anyone tell you otherwise, especially not yourself. The only difference between you and the person you look up to is the fact they had the courage to pull the trigger once they aimed.

Rejection is a part of life. Your idols have all been rejected at some point in life. Not a single toe that hits the ground is attached to a perfect human being. There are people born with talent but talent means nothing without effort. Anything can be learned and anything can be mastered with enough effort. Having talent is a bonus but it is neither necessary nor required in order to overcome rejection and get what you want. I had been told I would never lose weight and my response? I lost 150lbs and competed in a bodybuilding competition. I was rejected from all three colleges I applied to my senior year of high school and lived to see another day. Rejection can be a blessing in disguise and unfortunately, we have no way of knowing beforehand if it is a blessing or not. I was not ready for college at the time. If I had gotten accepted, I would not have found my best life and subsequently would not have written this book. Being knocked down is not a negative event but an empowering one. However, failing to get up from being knocked down is the negative event. Have the courage to get back up and move in a positive direction.

Break the rules by having the courage to live outside of the box. Follow your passions whether you have a clear path or intricate path. To find passion in life, sometimes it can involve luck. "If you're lucky enough, you'll find it early in life." (Kobe Bryant in Kobe: The Interview). Passions drive us to our best life. Without passion, life becomes colorless. An unappealing gray object left on the corner of a dinner plate being picked at with a fork by a person asking, "What is this?" Life needs passion as much as we need oxygen. Chase your wildest dreams in your pursuit of your best life.

You're not crazy for wanting to do so. Those who are courageous enough to chase are the ones who ultimately succeed, getting up twice as much as they get knocked down. We must comprehend passion as much as we must comprehend the implications courage has on life; it cannot survive without it.

Where do you want to be? This is an important question you need to ask yourself. Your vision of your best life should be as detailed as possible as if you were an anesthesiologist assistant. List out what you want in 6 months, 1 year, 2 years, etc. This should contain material wants and non-material desires. Refrain from hesitating to write your largest dreams regardless of how out of reach they may seem right now. There is no dream that is too big for your best life but to reach those lofty dreams, you must start now.

Little by little, make progress towards what you crave out of life. Where you begin, your old life ends. Have the courage to start, knowing your end result will look entirely different than your starting point and you can thank yourself later for starting sooner rather than hesitating. There are no rules when you're aiming to achieve your best life.

8

RIDE YOUR OWN WAVE

Throughout the journey of achieving your best life, you'll soon figure out you are your best hype man (or woman) and your worst enemy at the same time. Having the capability of pushing yourself beyond your wildest dreams but also preventing yourself from doing anything by using certain language and actions is power to the highest extent. Power, in the wrong hands, can resemble a two-year-old with a bowl of chocolate pudding in an all white room: messy and dangerous. With so much power in your hands, it is of necessity for you to pay attention to the language in which you use and the language others around you use.

At any point, have you ever asked someone why he or she were having a bad day and they then proceeded to tell you about something someone had said to them that pissed them off? The powers of the words used were so strong, it was able to disrupt and ruin that person's entire day. Imagine that, allowing the actions or language of someone else to ruin your entire day, is a shame. Twenty-four hours! The moment in question more than likely lasted for less than five minutes, which leaves you with a remaining twenty-three hours and five minutes to turn your day around with positive language and actions. The worst part is, the other person probably went about their day and didn't think twice about what transpired. Take a minute to remind yourself not to let a moment such as that effect your entire day and do something to reverse the mood it induced. There are not many instances where it is worth an entire day of your best life to be wasted.

Language is universal and transpires each second of the day. The most language being used comes non-verbally. This means even when we are not speaking, we are sending a message; make sure it is the right message. Your body language is a powerful tool that can elevate the energy in the room or bring it down. The same can be said for the people and atmosphere you surround yourself with. Ensure you keep yourself divulged in a positive atmosphere with people who bring positive vibes into your best life by using the friendventory you've created.

Others' language is important but not as important as your own. Achieving your best life is no easy feat and will need every bit of positive reassurance. Talk yourself up! Speak life into yourself if no one else will. Be slightly arrogant in a way. Boosting confidence in oneself can be hard at first if it is in trace amounts or non-existent but remember the notion actions beget feelings. When you act confident, you will begin to feel confident. You may have to create and ride your own wave in order for others to want to surf with you but first, you must be courageous enough to believe in yourself.

Building yourself up with positive language and confident actions will take multiple attempts. Life and surfing can be synonymous. There are plenty of waves in the ocean but you have to find the best fit for you. You can only find the best fit by trying to ride wave after wave. Falling off of your board but willing to fall again until you attain the best ride possible. Once you do, ride that momentum! Unfortunately, it is easier than ever these days to get distracted by other waves, which might look better than the one you are currently riding but we must remember, our wave is unique and only we can ride it with our special style.

Every person has their own wave. Every single person who reads this book has their own unique wave. My wave is different from yours but it does not mean yours is not as beautiful or not as great. It is your job to try to perfect the technique it requires to ride your own wave.

Online non-verbal language and actions, in the form of social media, can threaten our best life if we are not careful. Social media and FOMO (fear of missing out) dictate an unreasonable amount of activities some people may choose to do in their life. If an event is not worthy of a social media feed, some may not attend it. Without bragging rights to show for it, why bother to show people or experience it ourselves, right? That is a dangerous mindset to fall into. Allowing the perception or chance to impress others should never dictate how we live life. Unfortunately, most wake up and instantly scroll through social media and are blitzed with the glitz and glamour of other's "lives" which precedes us to evaluate our own and compare who has the better life. Your best life is neither better nor worse than anyone else's best life as each person holds a different definition for the term best but each life is great in his or her own rights. Life should be appreciated from all point of views rather than compared.

We fail to realize the photos being posted are simply highlights of a fabricated moment. Every person wants to put his or her best foot forward and social media is the perfect place to do so. Showing smiles, places, and objects to create status and display they are living a better life. Life is not always pure bliss and moments simply cannot be captured at all times. Your best life will be far too busy and exciting to remember to capture every moment, forcing you to be present in the moment, forgetting your phone exists, and constructing enough joyful stories for you to share with your friends later on. There are times when living through an experience outweighs living through a lens and your best life will be a perfect display of this sentiment.

On my recent trip to Hawaii, I had every intention to capture amazing photos while I was there. However, something happened that I was not expecting; I did not pick my camera up once except for the first day. While I wanted to capture the moments, there was no desire to have my camera out and furthermore; I was too busy having fun. I wanted to live in the moments with a huge emphasis on the word live. Without a camera or phone to distract me, I was able to meet a countless number of new people who later became friends and see a side of the island that I otherwise would not have, with absolute zero regrets of not showing it on social media. It is completely acceptable not to show every second of life and live.

Of course, everyone asked to see photos when I returned but to their surprise, I had very few to show. The expectation when visiting a beautiful island such as Hawaii is to take a billion travel photos and share them on social media to tell everyone how much of a great time you had. I had other plans. I wanted to share the experience in the form of a story shared amongst friends over dinner and that is exactly what I did.

Along with language, riding your own wave also entails going off the path and forming your own. When attempting to live your best life, sometimes it is necessary for us to venture off the path we are currently on by taking a break or even changing directions. Doing things that are not done the typical way or have not been done does not insinuate it is neither wrong nor right. It should also not deter you from doing them because it is simply your unique way of doing things and there is nothing wrong with that. Your best life is the same. It is unique like a wave in a large body of water containing other unique waves and can only be lived by you.

You are the most important person in your life and every fiber of your body deserves to know it. Do the things which bring you the most joy and use language that ignites fire in your soul. The power is in your hands to create a fortress and spread positivity.

9

EAT WELL, MOVE WELL, READ MORE, AND TRAVEL OFTEN

The wonderful joy of living is experiencing all of the pleasures this world has to offer. From amazing mouth-watering inducing food to breath taking sights, the culmination of unique viewpoints in the form of literature, and variety of cultures, life is meant for exploring. In order for us to experience all of the benefits in life, we must care for ourselves first. Treating your body and mind with respect and love is an essential part of achieving your best life but often overlooked.

Care for your body and mind as you would a brand new car. As a matter of fact, treat it like your favorite luxury sports car. You would never let the gas tank come close to becoming empty and you would never put cheap gas in such a fine automobile. You would want the car to run as efficiently as possible; always getting routine maintenance, washing and detailing the car, and trying not to get a scratch on it. If you'd treat a luxury sports car with so much care, why wouldn't you treat yourself the same? I'd like to think you're worth much more than a vehicle in which can be replaced.

With a car, it is nice and shiny at first but begins to accumulate wear and tear like a human body. However, when a car is well taken care of, it lasts years longer than similar cars that were not treated with care. The difference between a car and a human life is when the car finally sputters out, you can buy a new one to replace it. You cannot buy a new life or replace a life with a used model. You get one life and the one you are blessed with should be taken care of to the best of your abilities. Spend more on groceries, keep up with personal hygiene, be active, stimulate your mind, and expand your perception of the world.

Eat Well

"You are what you eat"
−Victor Lindlahr

When the time came for me to change directions in life, there were some undoubtedly noticeable changes I needed to make in order to do so. I had desires of eating the best food this world had to offer, move better than I was currently able to move and lead an active lifestyle, read more books to expand my knowledge and creativity, and travel to as many places as possible. It occurred to me the quality of food was just as important or I should say more important than what I the actual food I was consuming. What good is eating food if it doesn't make you feel good?

Eating more fruits, natural sugars, root vegetables, saturated fats, fewer grains, fewer muscle meats, and being more mindful of how certain foods made my body feel, changed my life forever. Attempting to eat more organic whole foods and grass-fed meats was something I ignorantly said was a joke. I was uneducated at the time and rightfully so.

The information, while available, is not shared as much as it should be in certain instances and has to be discovered through unbiased and open-minded research. The "healthy" food I was consuming prior simply was not as healthy as one would think. A diet high in protein, grains, and processed bars touted by the food industry to live a healthier life made me feel dead inside. Inflammation riddled my body and brain. Head fog became prevalent daily and body aches became expected. This was normal I thought because I had heard others complain of the same. How are we to know when we feel good if we continue to eat the same things that make us feel poor? Biting the bullet, I decided to give a new way of eating a try and within days, I felt amazing. This was a wake-up call and my best life was ready to answer.

The cost of the answer was and is still more expensive than the eating lifestyle I was previously leading but it is worth every cent. You may notice eating well also may mean spending more on groceries. The reason for the uptick in price comes from the time, labor, and popularity of certain foods. The longer the animal lives on the farm, every month it will cost the rancher more to feed and take care of the animal.

A higher price tag should not deter you. In fact, this can be a good thing. Choose to spend a little more on groceries and decrease your spending in other areas that may not be of as high importance. After all, we are all worth it so as the old saying goes: "Put your money where your mouth is".

Eating well entails more than simply eating healthy. Eating well means to enjoy delicious food but being conscious of the quality of foods we put in our body. Care for where your food comes from. What your food eats, is essentially what we will eat. If animals are fed grain and soy feed to fatten them up and prepare them for production, why would we ingest the same? I am not calling for you to go vegan, that is, of course, your choice, but achieving our best life assumes we are around to actually see and enjoy it so if animals are eating things to fatten them up/kill them, what do you think the result will be if we were to eat the same? Therefore, eating well goes hand in hand with your journey in your best life.

Move well

What we eat plays a major role in how well we move and also our willingness to move. Achieving your best life can't be accomplished from a chair or laying on the couch. It will require you to be active. The right foods will enhance our health, making it easier to do the things we love and make us happy. Whether it is in form of climbing a mountain to see a breath-taking sunrise, divulging in yourself in yoga, or becoming stronger in the gym, you'll need to possess the ability to move and move well.

Being active, as we all should know, has a positive impact on life. As little as walking 10 minutes every day or every other day can add years to your life, improve health, induce happiness, and assist in preventing degenerative diseases. When we visit the doctor, they tell us to be active by walking for 30 minutes at least 3 times a week. Why?

30 x 3= 90 minutes a week.
Divide that by 7 and you get about 12 minutes of walking per day.

Twelve minutes lands right in the middle of 10-15 minutes. By walking in this amount of time, it can reduce blood pressure, cholesterol, insulin dependence, the need for medication, and also help lose weight. All things of which should prolong your life.

According to a study published in the Archives of Internal Medicine, depression sufferers who took a daily walk showed just as much improvement in their symptoms as people on medication. This is not to say walking cures depression by any means. However, what walking does do, is by walking, our brain releases fun chemicals like serotonin, endorphins, and dopamine. Serotonin affects mood, sexual desire, appetite, sleep, memory, and temperature regulation. Low serotonin levels are connected with depression. Dopamine affects movement, emotional response and your ability to feel pleasure. Depletion of dopamine can lead to diseases such as Parkinson's, MS, and Alzheimer's.

Exercise, in general, can be beneficial. With that being said, however, there is such a thing as too much exercise. Exercise, especially heavy lifting, cause stress on the body. Stress, along with poor quality foods can be a lethal combination. Contrary to fitness enthusiasts who we look up to on social media platforms, working out 5-7 days a week is not healthy, especially when it becomes to feel like a chore. Mentally, it can cause a destructive pattern by becoming so obsessed you begin feeling guilty when you miss a workout or eating something that is not in your diet, rejecting offers to eat out with friends, and planning your entire week around your gym schedule. This, a sign things have gone too far, should be taken note of.

What is more important to you, being happy or

looking good? Obviously, the answer would be both but where do we draw the line between having a good balance and becoming obsessive? There are some who simply do not care how happy they are as long as they look great. I've met them and let me tell you, it is the saddest thing to hear being uttered out of living person's mouth. Those people are probably not reading this book.

Moving well entails finding a balance between the gym and life. Simply do what makes you happy. If you can only make it to the gym two days out of the week, then two days is ok. Try not to sweat the small stuff. There are a variety of other things you can do to be active such as taking a walk/run, going on a hike, indoor/outdoor rock climbing, indoor/outdoor sports, and etc. The goal of moving well is to become happier, lead an active lifestyle to prolong life, and enjoy the aforementioned delicious food. Find balance and have fun while enjoying moments of intense gut cramping laughter.

Read More

In a world illuminated by screens, it's good to focus the eyes on print every now and again (or a lot). If you had explained to me while I was growing up that I'd enjoy reading, I would have laughed in your face. As with most kids, I despised reading as much as kids despise veggies. The truth of the matter is, after picking up books that interested me, reading started to become enjoyable. Enjoyable, in the sense, I was looking forward to sitting down and diving into the next chapter. I was learning and with age, this idea became more exciting. After joining the "a chapter a day" train and finishing book after book, my thoughts had expanded in ways I hadn't anticipated. It is a huge reason as to why "read more" is a part of this book and should earn a place in your best life. If there's one thing that I hope you take away from this, it is to read more.

Reading makes you a better conversationalist. By reading, it broadens our vocabulary and contributes to you being more of an effective communicator. Those who tend to read often can typically express themselves in an array of ways. This can come in handy in many situations, especially while traveling.

Reading makes you smarter. We all have a tendency to be slightly closed minded on certain subjects. Reading allows for us to get more than one angle to how things work in this world. People who lean more towards the heavier side of reading have more of an open mind toward trying new things and ultimately discovering more effective ways to do things in life. In you can recall, this is a constant theme in achieving your best life.

Reading expands creativity. There's an indescribable feeling after you've finished a book that inspires you. Sometimes a good book within your interests can get the ball rolling on your creativity and spark changes in which you may be surprised. My best life and project "The Be Strong, Be Balanced Project" (www.dom-mitchell.com) didn't become what it is now until I read a few books, starting with The Happiness Project by Gretchen Rubin. Without creativity, we are unable to live passionately and without passion, we are not living our best life.

Reading can make you more attractive. This goes hand in hand with being a better conversationalist. Reading non-fiction books will allow you to expand your knowledge and put what you've read into your information vault. When a conversation arises around that topic, you can confidently add to the conversation rather than simply be nodding along. Being able to understand what is being said and adding more substance confidently is an incredible feeling and desirable trait. Who thinks a confident person in unattractive?

Reading will help you increase your focus. Reading forces us to shut out the outside world and focus on text. Zoning out in front of the television is great and has its purpose when you need something to let your brain rest after it's been fried but it doesn't help in the outside world. Think about the last thing you watched; does it have anything to do with your goals or have anything to do with achieving your best life? I can probably guess the answer. If you want to meet interesting people and enrich others lives, focus your attention towards a good book. A book in which will help you grow in the right direction. Reading itself is hard to focus on at first but with practice, it'll become easier and when a situation comes to where you must focus, you'll be able to apply that focus easily thanks to you reading more books.

Encouraging yourself to read more will benefit your best life in the long run. While I understand reading is not everyone's cup of tea, you should always be open to trying it out in order to discover if it is for you or not your thing. Start small with material that truly interests you. This could be a magazine or online blog post. The reasons stated above are personal findings after I chose I wanted to read more. It made me happy so therefore I continued to read more often than not. Read because you want to. Read because it is something you enjoy. If you do not enjoy what you are doing, there is no need to force yourself to do it.

Dom Mitchell

Travel Often

Let's face it, the world is such a large place filled with so many faces and places to see, that there is no humanly way possible to see it all in one lifetime. That being said, it's one more reason to travel. Confining your life to one place is doing a disservice to you and your best life. See as much as you possibly can and learn until you can no longer learn about cultures other than your own.

Learning about another culture helps your understanding of the world. It allows you to become more empathetic with those around you. By doing so, we can begin to end preconceived perceptions and create our own. Your efforts to be more open to learning about another culture and create your own perception may inspire someone else to do the same, inducing a ripple effect of positive progress in the world.

Traveling has many benefits. From providing you more happiness to sparking change in not only yourself but others as well. It is clear your best life can benefit from attempting to see as much of the world as possible by traveling because traveling provides excitement and unpredictability. Also, having friends of different cultures in different parts of the world gives you places to stay in future travel plans which is a huge bonus, knocking off costs to you and allowing you to spend your money on experiences. This is a no-brainer and a win-win situation if you ask me.

Taking care of yourself is of utmost importance, especially as it pertains to adding years to your best life. Give yourself the respect you deserve by eating better foods, staying active, reading when you can, and traveling as often as your heart desires. Your life is a life worth living.

10

LOVE THYSELF TWICE

"Distractions will do you in, in the truest sense"
-Drake

To get what you want out of your best life, it begins with how you start your mornings. While creating my best life, I made a rule called "2:1:1 ratio" and it was always to be done during my morning love time. It was designed to put me in the right mindset to start my day and also re train my brain to love twice as much as I loathed. Giving myself two compliments before firing off a negative comment or thought. These compliments don't have to be about your physical self but could be anything you truly enjoy about yourself. Do you love your sense of humor? Tell yourself you do aloud. Do you love your ability to solve other people's problems? Give yourself some credit! I found this behavior often difficult for people to adjust to but over time, becomes much more natural with practice. With there being enough judgment in the world as it is, there isn't a reason we should add to it by putting ourselves down.

What exactly is "morning love"? Tell me if this routine sounds familiar; wake up, grab the phone, reply to text messages/emails, scroll social media, go to the bathroom, continue to scroll... The problem with this routine is it does not involve you. We spend our first moments of a new day looking at others lives and jumping into conversations that may or may not be good for us to wake up to. Where is the time for the true star in this movie; you? We should always put ourselves first, especially in the morning. It allows us to shape who and what we want to attract. Focus on what you want from the day, the things that give you joy, the types of people you want to meet, the energy you want people to receive from you, and the things you are grateful for.

Reply Later

Every response does not deserve a response/reaction. At least not right away, anyway. If it is not urgent, try reading the message first but allowing yourself time to process your response before sending it back. We need to allow our minds to focus on us first and others second to give our best self to ourselves and to others.

Turn on Your Favorite Music

Turn on some upbeat music and let the brain get moving! Instrumentals are great in this situation. Not hearing any words other than your own thoughts can be more beneficial than you think. Without the influence of other's words, we are able to grasp our own thoughts, think clearly, and allow our bodies to respond to the rhythm. At times, words are necessary but you have to make the choice of what you need in the morning. A couple of my favorite stations on Spotify are "Summer Heat", "Lush Vibes", and "Hot Rhythmic" to get my days started.

Ask Questions

What makes you happy? Are you doing it? If you had the day off, what would you be doing? What do you want out of today? What are you grateful for? These are all examples of questions that should be asked often but especially in the morning. There should be no trouble in answering these and there is, more focus should be put on yourself to find who you truly are. The chapter "Be You" will explain more.

Meditate

Five minutes a day of meditation is all you need. Meditating has helped me by allowing me to remember small details about things, which in turn helped appreciate them more. I can remember every bit of how the waves sounded in Hawaii or how the sand felt in California as if I had just returned yesterday. We take advantage of things and people often. Take the time to get in touch with self, in order to appreciate every moment you have with others while you can. At some point, you'll be glad you did.

Not everyone gets to wake up the next day and not everyone is as fortunate as most of us are to be in the living situations that we are living in. Think about it; we woke up in a bed, with a roof over our head, a fridge full of food, can use a clean bathroom, can walk and see well, reading this book, etc. We are truly blessed. Take the time to appreciate that. Take the time to appreciate who you are. Be kind to yourself and others around you. Your best life is more than just being only about yourself, it is also about how you make people feel.

11

THE THREAT OF A SMILE

"Put your frown on before they think you soft. Never
smile long or take your defense off"
–J. Cole

"Be happy, it drives people crazy."

"Honestly, as long as you're happy, who the hell cares?"

How ironic is it to say a smile can be threatening? There
are many positive opinions of a smile, yet a smile is
perceived as a weakness instead of strength in certain
circumstances. Your smile is the key to your best life but
is a key constantly lost because it is not of high value in
some parts of our world. With a lot of controlling
expectations and influences, the presence of a smile
means more to the eye than you may think. Smiles can be
faked but the difference between a fake smile and
authentic one is the energy it brings.

A person who is happy from within cannot be
broken. This frightens people. There are people who
want to prove they are powerful in every situation. Prove
they are the alpha. Doing or saying anything they can to
break you down, attempting to put you in your place and

let it be known you are beneath them. You cannot do such a thing with a person who is truly happy. The alpha will fail, becoming angrier at every failed attempt, ultimately giving up trying to break this person because there is no joy if the other person cannot be fazed.

But why... why can a happy person not be broken? A person who is happy becomes confident in himself or herself. It takes work to find who you are and accept yourself regardless of anyone else's thoughts of you. Once you get to this point, there is no way you will ever go back. You have worked too hard to let someone take that away from you. Happiness builds a fortress with a positive reassuring force field around the love you have for yourself and constructs a team of snipers to sit on top of it, ready to pick anything off that comes close to threatening an unwanted entrance. Our happiness is a byproduct of the quality of our thoughts and mindset; a mindset is a tough thing to break or change.

Achieving your best life lies within how you view yourself first and foremost. The difference between those who are happy and those who are not is the ability to let every situation be what it is, instead of what you think it should be. In a negative situation that threatens your happy state, you have to two options. Either change the situation or change your mindset towards it.

Very little is needed to make your best life your happiest life; all you need to be happy is already inside of you and your way of thinking. You deserve to smile and smile genuinely. Happy people drive others crazy because those who are happy are strong. You are the alpha. Confidently live with no rules and smile as you're doing it.

12

POSITIVELY POSITIVE

One constant in all of our lives is gossip. It is quite possibly the hardest thing to escape. No matter where you turn, there is someone who wants to either entertain gossip and/or create it. Who doesn't want to know the juicy details about a coworker or the specifics of a popular breakup? While gossip may seem like a good idea at the moment, gossiping can at times, be a negative act. Gossip is usually to criticize or judge others and it brings about a sense of confirmation from those who are spreading the gossip. It builds a community of those who play by the same rules and ostracizes those who break them. Regardless of gender, we all like to gossip but does gossiping live in our best life?

Gossip can be fun and may even be necessary for some but it has no benefit to the overall goal here, which is your best life. Reading chapter after chapter and making positive changes to your life but only to gossip like you are in a high school girl's locker room, would be counterproductive to the progress you have made. Personally, when I decided to cut out gossip, I felt much lighter. Focus had shifted to self and negative language seemed to be cut in half. You don't know how much gossip inhibits your happiness until you erase it from the equation.

Even though I liked doing it, it never made me feel right. Making observations and commenting on them in a rude or uncalled for manner didn't make me cool or better than anyone else. In actuality, it made me worse. What had that person done to me in order to deserve such a negative comment? What impact does them wearing something that I personally wouldn't wear have on my life? What do I benefit from talking about and commenting on the details of someone else's life if it has no effect on my own? The answer was "nothing" in each instance. There is no way to spread positivity and negativity at the same time. If you find one, please email me with details.

Furthermore, gossip influences others' perception of people. If I were to tell you about the problems in my relationship, you will make a judgment about that person based on what was said, regardless if the two of you had met before or not. "Wow, I can't believe she would act that way". Instantly we set the other person up for failure. Everyone does not know each person on this planet, relying on word of mouth and "what do think of so and so", what we say about the unknown has greater implication than we may think. Give others the chance to make their own judgments based off of experiencing the person for themselves rather than experiencing them through gossip first.

Words are powerful and even if you meant no harm, you are never sure what emotions your gossip may bring. Every person has something they don't like about themselves or has something they have done in which they aren't exactly running to tell their grandparents about, why must you add to the fire? There is no way to know what is going on in someone else's life which means there is no reason for us to have a comment or to pass judgment. We may hear things but are they the truth? Our words should elicit smiles, generating an army and using the smiles as the weapon of choice.

Avoiding gossip may be arduous than not contributing to it. It is all around us! It's on the radio, on the Internet, on television, and on podcasts. Consumption of other's lives seems to be the focal point of conversations. Following celebrity's lives and relationships as if they were of kin. However, if we were living our best life, there would be no other focus because our lives would be too marvelous to want to focus anywhere else. With that being said, talking about another person's life, such as a celebrity or anyone else, will benefit your life in no way whatsoever. It's a waste of time and time is of delicacy or at least it should be if you're aiming to achieve your best life.

Adhere to positive gossip if possible. The negativity of gossip is not something your ears need to digest and quite frankly, is nothing you have time for if you're busy living your best life. Studies were performed and showed people unintentionally transfer traits said by one person to the other. This means if you were to talk poorly of someone to another person, that person would associate you with the negative qualities or comments even they already know you. Doesn't sound like a good perk to gossiping. I try my best to stay away from gossip, only speak highly of people, and live my best life. You should as well.

13

DECIDE. COMMIT. DO.

I get asked all of the time about how I am so sure about things or hear comments about how straightforward I am and know what I want. This was definitely not always the case. Ask my mother if you don't believe me. In fact, the changed happened on New Years Day in 2017. Mentally, the change had been happening for months internally. As it festered inside of my head, the reactions of others caused hesitation. Once I made the decision to go after what I wanted and be straightforward about it, committing to the decision, and simply did it, there was absolutely no going back to my old ways of procrastination and overthinking. I had completely changed overnight with the flip of a switch but this was only noticeable to an outsider. I, myself, knew who I was on the inside and what I wanted but always worried about how others would react or think. Enough was enough. It was time for me to start making decisions and commit to achieving my best life.

The idea here is for you to become familiar and become comfortable with decision-making, ending procrastination once and for all. Thinking about something for long periods of time is exactly like running on a treadmill; while it may get some things going internally, you don't actually get anywhere. Life will continue its course and will not wait for you to make a decision. The same thing you're procrastinating over may not be there when you finally decide to pull the trigger. There are things in life in which you will not be quite ready for and often times it will never be a good time for you to act. The truth is you'll never be completely ready if you continue to think about it and there will always be something in the way of making it the perfect time.

You simply need to go for it. Whatever it may be, do it and do it now. You may not be good at first but that's not the point. I have a friend, Jacob, who supposedly was going to start his journey at the same time I started mine with the goal we could help each other out along the way. I began but month after month, there was a different excuse as to why he hasn't begun. At the same time, month after month I was making further progress not because I was better but because by starting, I began learning and adapting, furthering my progression. Had I waited for him, my life would have never improved and therefore this book would not have been written. The take away is by deciding to do something, committing to it, and actually doing it, I made much more progress in a swifter fashion than I would have if I continued to sit around thinking about doing it.

Procrastination can come in the form of distractions by way of our phones or television. In no way am I calling for you to do a fire sale on your belongings or become Amish. What I am saying though is to turn off your phone and television for two hours simultaneously on a day of your choosing and observe how much you can accomplish. Quietness often brings about boredom, however, boredom breeds actions. It forces you to do something with your time rather than being distracted by the fabricated drama on the screen. With the screen on, our ears and eyes are also on, meaning if something in the background were to catch our attention, we would stop what it is we are doing to watch. If the distraction is not prevalent, there would be no other option than to enhance our focus, enabling us to make the most of our time. Furthermore, the quietness can promote actions of getting up and being active outside.

This step was a huge turning point for me as well. Once I rid myself of screens for a couple of hours, a number of tasks I completed were ridiculous. I remade my website, took online courses, wrote two guides for my project, had five photo shoots, updated my portfolio, and this was in the first two weeks! By the end of the first month, I had written so many blog posts, I was on autopilot for months, which gave me time to write this book in the second month. By choosing to fully commit my time towards myself, it created wonderful opportunities and a fresh outlook on my best life. There was no looking back.

It was time to step with purpose, act with intent, and waste less movement. Creating small tasks such as checking email, social media, cleaning that small spot of toothpaste on the mirror, simply is us procrastinating and mastering it with tasks may not seem like much. Swipe left too much and you'll notice an hour has passed with no improvement to the original goal. If we simply were to focus our full attention on the task at hand instead of finding ways not to do it, we'd save ourselves a lot of time and accomplish a lot more things than we may think. Let's be honest here; accomplishing a task early feels good! Getting that project out of the way early will allow for downtime later. Downtime in which can be used to do things that make you happy.

14

FALL FORWARD

"I can accept failure, everyone fails at something. But I
can't accept not trying."
-Michael Jordan

"You miss 100 percent of the shots you never take."
–Wayne Gretzky

How many times a person fails is not as important as
how they fail. Failing is how we learn best. It can be
argued we only learn by failing but failing is a scareful
event to most that is often avoided like the plague. In life,
there will always be set backs and downfalls but it is not
indicative of how well one may live his or her life. There
is no way around failure. The ideology of perfection
cannot exist without failure. With this being said, I urge
you to want to fail, embracing it as much as you possibly
can because to achieve your best life, you will need to fail
multiple times and not only fail but fail with joy.

To simply fail for the sake of failing is not what I
mean here. Fail in order to progress. Fail in order to learn.
Fail better than you had previously by taking the failure
and using what you've learned to progress in future
endeavors. Failing means that you tried something but it

didn't work this time around or it simply was not the right time. While in the grand scheme of things it may not have worked this time around, there are often small events that are looked over that may have been positive in the situation.

For example, my blog can be considered a failure to most. It does not generate income nor does it generate thousands of subscribers which most people would consider that to be a failure. But it is not a failure. The things in which I've learned about what works and what does not is irreplaceable. Blogging is much more than a simple website with some text, blogging is something I truly enjoy doing because it is an outlet of the project. I would not have known what to do or how to turn it into a success without being open to failure.

When I began the "Be Strong, Be Balanced Project", I had absolutely no traffic whatsoever. I thought I had done everything I could do and no one seemed to be coming to my site. However, I did not let that stop me. Slowly but surely I began to learn the ropes and those few people became 25. Those 25 people rose to 100. The 100 ballooned to 1000. Before you knew it, I had a made some decent traction. But this is not the reason it is not a failure in my eyes. Writing on the blog makes me happy and is apart of this project regardless if someone sees it or not, it was made for me and had I not have failed in the beginning, I wouldn't have learned how to improve while mitigating minor mistakes.

Every person is subject to making mistakes at some point in time. It is an inevitable part of life. One thing to remember after making a mistake: You are not the first person to screw up and damn sure will not be the last. At times our mistake may carry a negative connotation and free ourselves from the process of holding onto our mistakes, will only bring about positive vibes. There is absolutely nothing wrong with admitting to making a mistake or failing, it only means you are a mere mortal and not some super hero walking among us. This is life and you are only human. Again, 90 percent of things can be reversed in life so there is no need to beat yourself up for living. The only question that comes from making a mistake or failing is what are you going to do next?

The goal of falling forward is to make progress towards your best life. Renounce your old feelings towards failure and open your mind to enjoying the process. The process is often the best part of the journey. The old saying: It is not about the destination in life but the journey is a great way of letting you know you are not alone in life. Have fun with it! There is not a reason to become upset as everything happens for a reason. It may seem tough whilst in the moment but you have to put trust in self to get past it.

Think of yourself as a baseball player. Playing under the bright lights with everyone watching as you step up to bat as the sweat begins to drip uncontrollably. You're at the plate and your best life is pitching. Without knowing what pitch is coming towards you, you need to prepare and practice swinging at all types of pitches. Deciding how and when you're going to swing, amongst other things crosses your mind in an instance. It's ok to bunt but you're trying to hit it out of the park, right? This is your best life so swing for the fences! Whatever you do, do not let a pitch go by without a swing, leaving the plate with "what if's" and "I should haves" should not be accepted. A batter, who does not swing does not hit a home run and a batter who does not strikeout does not learn.

Is failing necessary? I believe it is. I once prided

myself on being a perfectionist but being a perfectionist is tiring; it means nothing will ever be good enough and is subject to change as we gain new perspectives about our definition of perfection. However, once I realized perfection meant being imperfect, my perception of failing changed. Striving for perfection meant there would always be room for improvement with growth but that was the beauty of the pursuit. To make changes would insinuate the previous attempt was not working or something was found that could be improved upon. With every tweak or change, it meant that I was admitting to failing previously but aiming to fail better this time around by striving for "perfection". Perfection is failing and improving at the same time. Your best life is no different. You will fail in your attempt to achieve it but with every attempt, you will also improve significantly.

Dom Mitchell

15

FINAL WORDS

Life is tough! Achieving your best life is may quite essentially be tougher. There will be missteps along the way but there will also be a great success while attempting to live your own way. Be kind to yourself as well as others and help those who may need it along the way. Remember, we can do anything we want in life as long as fear is welcomed by our confidence and courage. There is only one you in this world and that person deserves the absolute best. No one can be you better than you can be you.

You have the ability to make a huge impact on not only those around you but to your younger self, your future self, and those who will come after you. How are you inspiring others to live their best life? How do you find your passion and use that passion to inspire someone else to create their passion, passing that on to the next person? Your answer lies within your best life.

STRIVE FOR HAPPINESS.

Spread positivity.

Live.

Salud!

ABOUT THE AUTHOR

(Dom)inique Mitchell is an entrepreneur and student with a strong passion for kinesiology, photography, food, reading, travel, and most importantly, happiness. The "Be Strong, Be Balanced Project" and the book "Living In Color", is his journey to achieve the "perfect" individual balance with the happiness of life. With a background in nutrition and a desire to learn, he wants to teach and inspire others around the world of those findings by sharing through actions as well as literature. Happiness doesn't end, therefore this project will be ongoing. He's on a journey to find those who wish to do the same or who simply want to follow his pursuit of achieving his best life. It doesn't have to be and most certainly won't be perfect by any means but it will be fun, exciting, and rewarding.

Naturally a happy person, recently Dom noticed more negativity and lack of happiness than he'd like to admit. At times, life felt completely at a standstill. He knew there was more to life than what he was doing. He wanted to eat better than he was, move better than he could currently, read more books to expand the mind, and travel to create new memories and friendships.

He grew up in a culture to which he felt as if his views were not how others saw the world. There are no rules to life but he knew he was a little different from the people around him. This is his journey to achieving his best life.

Dom Mitchell

"There are two types of people in this world; those who shoot and keep their eye on the goal and those who shoot and only pay attention to how they shot at the goal."

Dom Mitchell

Made in the USA
Lexington, KY
24 September 2017